PIP AND BUNNY: BUNNY VISITS LONDC

The invaluable 'Pip and Bunny' collection is a set of six picture books with an accompanying handbook and e-resources carefully written and illustrated to support the development of visual and literary skills. By inspiring conversation and imagination, the books promote emotional and social literacy in the young reader.

Designed for use within the early years setting or at home, each story explores different areas of social and emotional development. The full set includes:

- six beautifully illustrated picture books with text and vocabulary for each
- a handbook designed to guide the adult in using the books effectively
- 'Talking Points' relating to the child's own world
- 'What's the Word?' picture pages to be photocopied, downloaded or printed for language development
- detailed suggestions as to how to link with other EYFS areas of learning.

The set is designed to be used in both individual and group settings. It will be a valuable resource for teachers, SENCOs (preschool and reception), Early Years Staff (nursery, preschool and reception), EOTAs, Educational Psychologists, Counsellors and Speech Therapists.

Maureen Glynn has 25 years' experience teaching primary and secondary age children in mainstream, home school and special school settings, in the UK and Ireland.

First published 2020
by Routledge
2 Park Square, Milton Park, Abingdon, Oxon OX14 4RN

and by Routledge
52 Vanderbilt Avenue, New York, NY 10017

Routledge is an imprint of the Taylor & Francis Group, an informa business

British Library Cataloguing-in-Publication Data
A catalogue record for this book is available from the British Library

Library of Congress Cataloging-in-Publication Data
A catalog record for this book has been requested

ISBN: 978-0-367-19020-0 (pbk)
ISBN: 978-0-367-37541-6 (ebk)

Typeset in Calibri
by Apex CoVantage, LLC

Visit www.Routledge.com/9780367136642

Book 3 Bunny Visits London

Whilst Pip is in school, her daddy has a meeting in London.
His name is Ben.

He travels by train to Paddington Station. Bunny goes too.

Bunny enjoys the ride on the Underground Tube train.

There are so many people.

In London, Bunny hops out of Ben's coat pocket
and spies a toy shop...

She has never seen so many toys and games to play with.

She hops and hops on, to visit the London Eye.

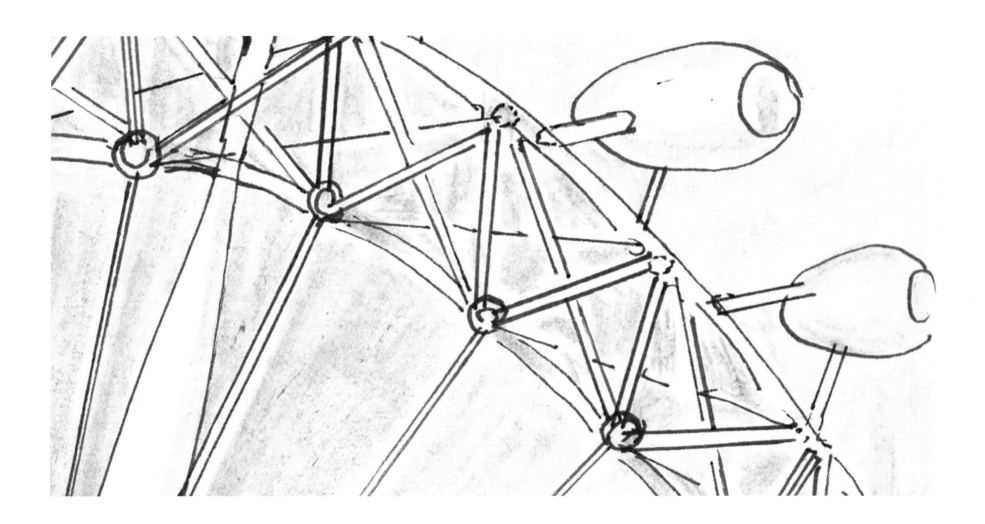

She takes a ride.

'Wheee, this is fun!' she yells.

Then Bunny hops onto a big red London bus.

She spots Big Ben and…

Watches the guards at Buckingham Palace.

Now it is time to go home.

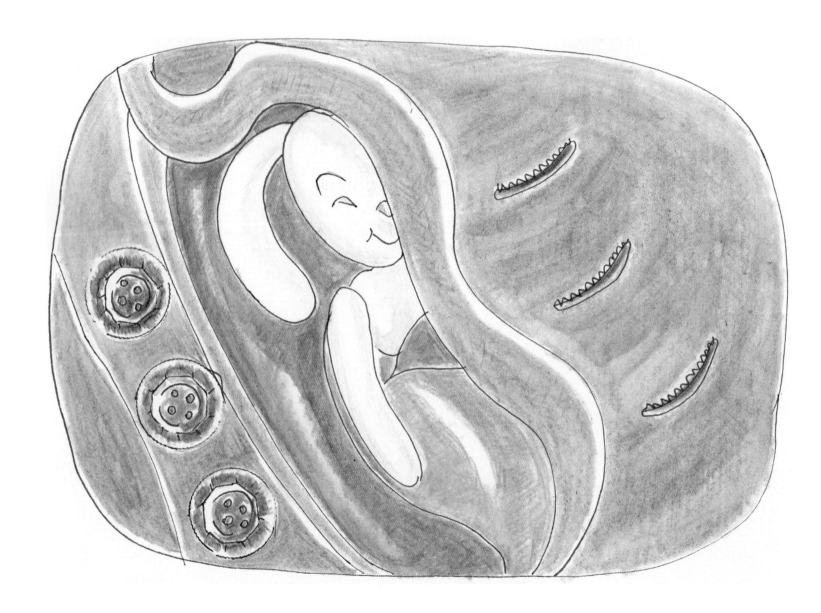

Bunny has had a wonderful day!

Can you tell Pip all about Bunny's visit to London?

Book 3 Bunny Visits London What's the Word?

Show the page and ask the child to say words that explain each image:

Page 18 Action Words?

Page 19 Location Words?

Page 20 Descriptive Words?

Page 21 Transport Words?

Page 22 Emotions and Feelings?

Action Words?

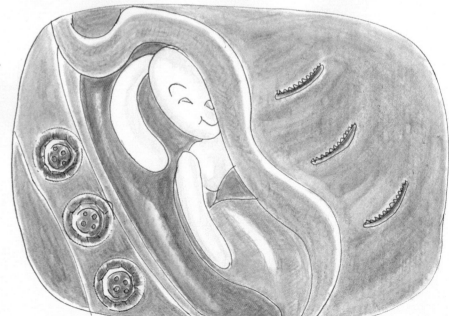

Location Words?

Descriptive Words?

Transport Words?

Emotions and Feelings?